Jane Annie;
Or, The Good
Conduct Prize

Jane Annie;
Or, The Good
Conduct Prize

J.M. Barrie and
Sir Arthur Conan Doyle

MINT EDITIONS

Jane Annie; Or, The Good Conduct Prize was first published in 1893.

This edition published by Mint Editions 2021.

ISBN 9781513281360 | E-ISBN 9781513286389

Published by Mint Editions®

MINT
EDITIONS

minteditionbooks.com

Publishing Director: Jennifer Newens
Design & Production: Rachel Lopez Metzger
Project Manager: Micaela Clark
Typesetting: Westchester Publishing Services

Dramatis Personae

A Proctor
Sim (Bulldog)
Greg (Bulldog)
Tom (a Press Student)
Jack (a Warrior)
Caddie (a Page)
Miss Sims (a Schoolmistress)
Jane Annie (a Good Girl)
Bab (a Bad Girl)
Milly (an Average Girl)
Rose (an Average Girl)
Meg (an Average Girl)
Maud (an Average Girl)

Schoolgirls, Press Students, and Lancers.

*The Scene is obviously laid round the corner from a certain
English University Town.*

Act I
First Floor of a Seminary for the Little Things that grow into Women.

Act II
A Ladies' Golf Green near the Seminary.

Time
The Present.

One Night elapses between the Acts.

*The Opera produced under the Stage Direction of Mr. Charles Harris and the
Musical Direction of Mr. Francois Cellier.*

* Caddie's explanatory notes are included in an appendix and indicated
in the text by numbers in square brackets [ ] that correspond to the
point in the libretto where they appear.

Act I

Scene.—*First floor of the Ladies' Seminary. The* Girls *are exchanging their last confidences for the night. Enter* Caddie[1] *with their candles.*

Chorus of Girls.

Good-night! Good-night!
  The hour is late;
Though eyes are bright,
  No longer wait!
Though clear the head,
  Though wit may shine,
To bed! To bed!
  It's nearly nine!

Dining-room clock strikes.

Milly: Now the last faint tint has faded.

All: Good-night! Good-night!

Milly: And the west in gloom is shaded.

All: Good-night! Good-night!

Milly: See the moon her vigil keeping.

All: Good-night! Good-night!

Milly: Torpor o'er the earth is creeping

All: Good-night! Good-night!

Drawing-room clock strikes.

All: Good-night! Good-night!
    A-talking thus,
  Though eyes are bright,
    Is not for us.
  The eve is past,
    The shadows fall,
  And so at last
    Good-night to all.

All retire except Caddie, *who is roused from a profound reverie by the misbehaviour of the clock. He makes short work of it. Exit* Caddie.[2] *There is a knock at the door, and the* Girls *reappear.*

Meg: It was the front door!

MILLY: Who can be calling at such a fearsomely late hour as nine o'clock?

ROSE: Why doesn't some one peep down the stairs.

BAB *runs downstairs.*

MAUD: That bold Bab has gone. Miss Sims will catch her.

MILLY: Oh! I can see. (*Looks over staircase*)

ALL: Well?

MILLY: A man!

ROSE: At last!

MILLY: Bald!

ROSE: The wretch!

MILLY: He has two other men with him.

MEG: Two! Girls, let us go and do our hair this instant.

MILLY: They are shewn into Miss Sims's private room. Ah!

MAUD: What?

MILLY: The door is shut.

ROSE: What a shame!

MEG: What is Bab doing all this time?

MILLY: She has her ear at the keyhole.

MAUD: Dear girl!

MILLY: She shakes her fist at the keyhole.

ALL: Why?

MILLY: I don't know.

BAB *comes upstairs.*

ROSE: Bab, why did you shake your fist at the keyhole?

BAB: Because it is stuffed with paper.[3]

ALL: Oh!

BAB: Yes, stuffed. How mean of Miss Sims. She might surely have trusted to our honour not to look.

MILLY: Thank goodness, the holidays begin the day after tomorrow.

BAB: But a great deal may happen before to-morrow. Girls, can you keep a secret—a secret that will freeze your blood and curl you up and make you die of envy?

ALL: Yes, yes!

BAB: That little sneak Jane Annie is not here?[4]

MILLY: She has gone upstairs to bed.

BAB: You are sure?

ROSE: I'll make sure. (*Runs upstairs and looks through keyhole*) It's all right, girls! I can see her curling her eyelashes with a hairpin.

GIRLS *surround* BAB.

BAB: Then, girls, what do you value most in the world?

MILLY: My curls.

MEG: My complexion.

ROSE: My diamond ring.

MAUD: My cousin Dick.

BAB: Well, Meg would be delighted her complexion fair to doff,
   And Milly take her scissors and cut her tresses off,
   And Rose with a careless "Take it" give up her diamond quick,
   And Maud would soon surrender her rights in Cousin Dick,
   To be me to-night!

MILLY: What is his name?

BAB: Jack.

MAUD: A lovely name! What are you and Jack to do?

JANE ANNIE *steals downstairs.*

BAB: This very night we have—

ALL: You have—?

BAB: Arranged to el—

ALL: To el—(*seeing* JANE ANNIE) Oh!

JANE ANNIE *comes forward. All turn their backs on her.*

JANE A.: What have you arranged to do to-night, Bab? What is it,
   Maud? tell me, Milly.

ROSE: You used to be the worst girl in the school, Jane Annie, and I
   believe you have become a sneak to win the good-conduct prize.[5]

MILLY: When it is presented to her to-morrow, I shall hiss.

JANE A.: What is your secret, Bab?

BAB: Oh, I should like to pinch you!

JANE A.: Just because I am a good girl.

SONG.—JANE ANNIE.

I'm not a sneak for praise or pelf,
   But when they're acting badly,
I want to make them like myself,
   And so I tell tales gladly.
      Just because I am a good girl.

ALL: She gives her reasons thus,
   But it's rather hard on us,
      To suffer just because she is a good girl.

JANE ANNIE: I told Miss Sims they read in bed,
　　Although with guile they cloaked it,
　And when her cane chair vanished,
　　I told her they had smoked it,
　　　And all because I am a good girl.

ALL: And all because she is a good girl.

JANE ANNIE: Although misunderstood, I'm meek—
　　Bab, pinch me, pinch me well!

(BAB *pinches her*)

Thanks! Next I offer you my cheek.

(BAB *slaps her*)

　Now, dear, I'll go and tell.
　　And just because I am a good girl.

ALL: She gives her reasons thus,
　But it's rather hard on us,
　　To suffer just because she is a good girl.

JANE A.: If I liked I could make Bab tell me her secret. Beware! I have a power by which, if I chose to use it, I can make any one do anything I like.

MILLY (*scoffing*): Then why don't you use it?

JANE A.: Because I am a good girl.

Exit JANE ANNIE *downstairs.*

ROSE: Do you think she has such a power?

MILLY: Of course not.

MEG: Still, Jane Annie could not tell a lie.

MILLY: You mistake. It was George Washington who could not tell a lie.

MEG: So it was. How stupid of me.

MAUD: Quick, Bab, your secret?

ALL: Yes—the secret!

BAB: Girls, this is my secret. Meg, watch! Jack is a soldier, and he loves me.

ALL: Oh!

BAB: But better still—I have two lovers.

MILLY: Do they hate each other?

BAB: Yes.[6]

MILLY: Scrumptious!

BAB: And, oh girls! I have promised to elope with Jack to-night.

ALL: Oh! (BAB *sighs*)

ROSE: But why do you sigh?

BAB: Ah, there is Tom, dear Tom! What is poor Tom to do?

ROSE: Then it is Tom you love?

BAB: Oh, I do not know which I love. Tom is so poor, and Jack is ready to take me now. Besides, I have promised.

MAUD: Then Jack has money?

BAB: He says he has a little.

MILLY: Only a little? Then what are you to live on?

BAB: Oh, we have worked that out very carefully. First of all he is to sell out. Then he has a friend who wrote a novel in six weeks and got £1,000 for it. Well, Jack has much more ability than his friend, so he is to adopt novel writing as a profession, and, as £1,000 in six weeks comes to £8,666 13s. 14d. a year, we shall be quite comfortable.

MILLY: I see you have left nothing to chance.

BAB: No.

ROSE: Where are you and Jack to meet?

BAB: All day I have been expecting a note to say if I am to meet him in the garden or on the tow path.

MISS SIMS[7] *and* JANE ANNIE *come up the stairs listening.*

MEG: H'st!

BAB (*softly*): Girls, we are watched! I must deceive the eavesdroppers. (*Aloud*) Girls, this is my secret about which you have asked me.

ALL: Ahem! Ahem!

SONG.—BAB.

Bright-eyed Bab I used to be,
    Now these eyes are lead;
Languor has come over me,
    Hangs my little head.
Now my figure—once like this—
    Droops like autumn berry;
Pity me, my secret is,
    Me is sleepy very!

ENSEMBLE.

MISS SIMS and GIRLS.	JANE ANNIE.
See her little drowsy head,	Does her naughty little head

Droops like autumn berry;   Droop like autumn berry?
Says she wants to go to bed,   Says she wants to go to bed,
    She is sleepy, very!   But I add a query?

BAB: Simple Bab is charged with art,
    Watched by cruel parties;
Palpitates her 'ittle heart,
    'Is where 'ittle heart is!
Something Bab has planned to do,
    Something will not keep;
Bab's a drowsy girlie who
    Has planned to—go to sleep.

ENSEMBLE.

MISS SIMS and GIRLS.	JANE ANNIE.
Such a guileless little head	Though she be a drowsy head,
Secret could not keep;	That is rather steep;
Tuck her in her cosy bed,	Tho' we tucked her up in bed,
And she'll go to sleep.	Would she go to sleep?

Exeunt GIRLS *slowly to refrain of* "Good-night, Good-night!"[8]

MISS S. (*to* JANE ANNIE): This explanation of Bab's seems quite
satisfactory.

JANE A.: Hum!

MISS S.: Bab, to bed.

BAB: Can't I stay up for a little, Miss Sims, to entertain your guests?

MISS S.: Insolence! I shall see you to your room.

BAB: I can hear them coming upstairs.

JANE A.: Do tell me who they are. I am not curious. I only want to
know.

MISS S.: They are the Proctor and his Bulldogs.

Exeunt MISS SIMS, BAB, *and* JANE ANNIE.

Enter PROCTOR *and* BULLDOGS.

RECITATIVE.—PROCTOR.

There was a time when we were not,
The name that this dark period got
    Was Chaos.
      It lay as 'neath a ban,

Merely containing animals, vegetables, minerals,
    Woman and the like, and man.
Said Nature, I've no Proctor,"
This strange omission shocked her.
Too long she felt she'd waited;
    She now enlarged her plan.
We Proctors were created,
    And then the world began.

SONG.—PROCTOR.

I'll tell to you what 'tis we do,
    We stalk the undergrad.
When he perceives our velvet sleeves,
    He runs away like mad.
Then follow we by deputy,
    These men I now describe;
My bulldogs sound pull him to ground,
    They never take a bribe.
In vain he tries to dodge their eyes,
    Of all his haunts they've knowledge;
And soon I make our quarry quake
    By crying, "Name and college!"
ALL: Name and college! Name and college!

PROCTOR: Caged lions may forget they're tame,
    The wife forget her baby's name,
    The trampled worm forget to turn,
    The Scot to think of Bannockburn,
    One poet in a score forget
    The laureateship is open yet,
    But none who of its gist have knowledge
    Can e'er forget my "Name and college."

In after years I fill with fears
    All who've been undergrads;
The Cabinet, the Laureate,
    Still run from me like lads.
To Parliament I one time went

The front bench to enlighten,
I thought I'd try to prove that I
    Could still the members frighten.
So up I rose, and struck the pose,
    And shouted, "Name and college!"
Oh, run did they from me that day,
    When I cried "Name and college!"

ALL: Name and college! Name and college!

PROCTOR: Comedians may forget their part,
    Librettists that it rhymes with heart;
    Composers may themselves forget
    When ragged rhymes they're asked to set;
    The Savoy opera singer e'en
    Forget that on his head he's been;
    But none who of its gist have knowledge,
    Can e'er forget my "Name and college."

(*Re-enter* MISS SIMS) JANE ANNIE *listens from balcony.*

MISS S.: Dear friend, you have not yet told me the reason for this visit, and I cannot hope that you have called merely because of our old friendship.

PROCTOR: Our more than friendship.

They sigh. BULLDOGS *sigh, and* PROCTOR *glares at them.*

GREG (*rebelliously*): We have our feelings.

PROCTOR: But I object to your having feelings.

SIM (*signing to* GREG *to control himself*): Then we haven't.

PROCTOR: Are they still following me?

GREG AND SIM (*going to window*): They are gone!

PROCTOR: Ha!

MISS S.: What is it, dear friend?

PROCTOR: It is the penalty of greatness. You have heard that a Chair of New Journalism has been established at the University. There has been no peace for me since. The Press Students follow me, interview me, describe me. You see, honours can now be got in this department, and they are all anxious to take the first "first class" in journalism.

GREG: Besides, they feel that if they don't hurry up, some lady student will take it before them.

MISS S.: It is a way that lady students have.

PROCTOR: But it was duty brought me here. I have private information that an undergraduate named Findlater—popularly known as Tom, is carrying on a—a—a—

GREG: A flirtation.

PROCTOR: A—a flirtation—(*He is reluctant to take the word from* GREG, *but can think of no other.* GREG *is triumphant.*)—with a certain—certain—one of these—ah! what do you call those little things that grow into women?

GREG: A girl.

PROCTOR (*annoyed*): A—a—girl—in this seminary.

MISS S.: Impossible! Could it be Bab?

GREG: Bab was the name.

PROCTOR *glares at* GREG, *with whom* SIM *expostulates in dumb show.*

JANE A. (*aside*): Tom! Tom! But I am sure the naughty word I heard her say was Jack! (*Exit* JANE ANNIE)

PROCTOR: Tom is coming to serenade her from this hall window. Now I have come here to watch, and if he is guilty, to have him sent down. Ha! ha! conceive his discomfiture when he climbs up to this window and is met—not by his sweetheart—but my cry of—

GREG: Name and college.

SIM (*quaking*): I don't know what is to become of him! (*To* GREG) Don't be so dashed independent!

PROCTOR (*fiercely*): Watch at the windows!

BULLDOGS *go to windows.*

MISS S.: Dear friend, you must be mistaken.

PROCTOR: Mistaken? I am a Proctor. Besides, if you are so confident, you cannot complain of my putting the matter to the proof, and I propose watching here. Where can I hide?

MISS S. (*pointing to clock*)[9]: Do you think you could get into this?

PROCTOR: The clock! Why not? I can just do it.

MISS S.: Good. And I shall watch downstairs, for I know that my school can triumphantly stand the test.

DUET.—MISS SIMS and PROCTOR.

MISS SIMS: Strictly tended plants are mine,
    Breakfast early, bed at nine—

PROCTOR: Plants that need some watching.

MISS SIMS: Their regard for beauty slight is,
   Mental charm their chief delight is—
PROCTOR: Mischief ever hatching.
MISS SIMS: Flirt's a word at which they frown,
   Man they know is but a noun—
PROCTOR: A noun they can't decline.
MISS SIMS: Eyes they never use amiss,
   When they take the air like this,
      In a maiden line. (*Business*)
PROCTOR: Yet I take this information
   With some mental reservation,
   And I think it most imprudent,
   Thus to fire the callow student,
      Or the young divine.
MISS SIMS: Helpful books they read—not Gyp,
   But the courting scenes they skip—
PROCTOR: Or at least they say so.
MISS SIMS: If the heroine who charms
   Sinks into her lover's arms—
PROCTOR: They hope to be some day so.
MISS SIMS: No, their comment prim and terse is,
   Namely "What a hard plight hers is!"
PROCTOR: Oh, this is quite too fine!
MISS SIMS: And mankind with scorn they view,
   As they walk out two and two,
      In a maiden line.   (*Business*)
ENSEMBLE:
   { MISS SIMS: Yet he takes my wise instructions
   {   With considerable deductions;
   {   For such sights are bad, I know
   {   For the budding medico,
   {   Or the young divine.
   { PROCTOR: Yet I take Miss Sims' instructions
   {   With considerable deductions;
   {   For such sights are bad, I know
   {   For the budding medico,
   {   Or the young divine.
GREG: Thank you so much. What is that called?

J.M. BARRIE AND SIR ARTHUR CONAN DOYLE

Miss S.: It is a little thing of my own.

Greg: How delightful!

Miss S.: I am so glad you like it.

Greg: You sing with so much expression.

Miss S.: Do you really think so?

Greg: Won't you favour us with another?

Miss S.: That is the only one I know.

Greg: How very charming! (Proctor *orders him back to window*)

Proctor: Ah me! Neither of us has forgotten the days when we were
lovers. What a pity we quarrelled!

Miss S. (*questioningly*): I suppose we have quite outgrown that
affection?

Proctor: Oh, quite. (Bulldogs *at the window make signs as if they
saw someone. Soft flute is heard outside*) Ah! he comes! It is Tom!
(Proctor *gets into the clock*, Miss Sims *assisting him.* Proctor
looking out) How's that?

Miss S.: Wonderful! If the face had hands you could pass for the clock
any day. And here they are. (*Puts her spectacles on* Proctor) There!
and now I shall watch downstairs.

Proctor: Hi! a moment. What have you set me at?

Miss S.: Ten past nine. (*Exit*)

Proctor: Now the minute hand is in my left eye and I can see
nothing. I wish she had put me on half an hour.

Greg (*coming down*): I beg to inform you, sir—he's gone! Sim, where
can the Proctor have vanished to?

Sim (*coming down*): I am glad he isn't here. What is to be done? We
didn't see what the Proctor expected us to see.

Greg: Is that our fault?

Sim: Hush! Of course it is, Greg. You will say we saw the
undergraduate, eh, Greg?

Proctor (*aside*): What?

Greg: But we didn't. It was a soldier we saw.

Proctor (*aside*): Eh?

Sim: Oh, what is to be done?

Greg: Tell him the truth.

Sim: Oh, Greg, don't be so independent! Think of the time when you
were a little child on your mother's knee.

(Greg *is much affected*)

DUET.—SIM and GREG.

SIM: When a bulldog I became,
　　Independence was my game,
　　But since my course I'm steering
　　　By a rule that is more wise,
　　For I hear with other's hearing,
　　　And I see with other's eyes.
GREG (*derisively*): Tooral, looral-ly!
SIM: That's a risky think to say.
GREG: It's my platform, I reply.
SIM: Platforms, Greg, are cheap to-day.
GREG: Which nobody can deny.
　　Man's a man for a' that, Sim.
SIM: For a what? say I,[10]
GREG: For a that.
SIM: A that? what's that?
GREG (*after reflecting*): Tooral, looral-ly!
BOTH: Up with caps and freedom hail!
　　　Here's the new election cry;
　　Man's a man if born a male,
　　　Tooral, looral, looral-ly!
GREG: Proc's are spry, but I see through them!
　　I'm the man that will undo them!
　　With a wit like razors' edges,
　　　Twit them in the 'Varsitee;
　　This the thin edge of the wedge is,
　　　Spell them with a little p.
SIM (*derisively*): Tooral, looral-ly!
GREG: Culture's fudge—see how I flout it,
SIM: Culture doesn't pay, that's why;
GREG: We reformers do without it,
SIM: Which nobody can deny.
GREG: Mad you are, my friend, go to!
SIM: Go to where? say I,
GREG: The missing word I leave to you.
SIM (*after reflecting*): Tooral, looral-ly!
BOTH: Up with caps and freedom hail!
　　　Here's the new election cry;

Man's a man if born a male,
  Tooral, looral, looral-ly!

DANCE.

Boots are placed outside the doors at this point. The BULLDOGS *look scared, and exeunt downstairs.*

Enter CADDIE. *He collects boots in a laundress's basket.*[11] *The boots he loves are not among them. He is distressed.* JANE ANNIE's *door opens and she puts out her boots. He is elated and goes for them. While he is getting them* BAB's *arm appears outside her door, groping for her boots. As she doesn't find then she comes out and looks for them. She sees basket, glides to it unseen by* CADDIE, *picks out her boots and exit with them.* CADDIE *returns with* JANE ANNIE's *boots, fondling them. He sits down on basket and kisses them. Then he rises and tries to drop them among the others. This strikes him as sacrilege. He shakes his head, then ties the laces of* JANE ANNIE's *boots together, slings them over his head, and exit, carrying basket.*

PROCTOR: What is he up to? If I had only being going, I should be at the half-hour by this time, and then I could see with the left eye. Ten past nine! I little thought that the time would come when the grand ambition of my life would be to be nine-thirty. What is he doing upstairs? Hello! a girl, and after some mischief. I wonder if I dare ask her to put me on twenty minutes. I feel very queer, as if I was turning into a real clock. I hope I sha'n't strike.

ROSE *and* MILLY *come softly out of their rooms.*

MILLY: I have been thinking so much of what Bab told us that I can't go to bed.

ROSE: Nor I—Oh, Milly!

MILLY: What time is it, Rose?

ROSE (*holding candle to clock*): Half-past nine.

PROCTOR (*aside*): I wish it was!

ROSE (*to* MILLY): What?

MILLY: I didn't speak.

Flute heard outside.

ROSE: Listen!

MILLY: Oh, Rose! I am all of a tremble; turn up the gas.

BAB *enters. Flute playing continues.*

ROSE: It is he—Jack!

BAB (*trembling*): No, that is Tom!

MILLY: The other one!

BAB: Milly, he must have heard that I am to elope with Jack and doubtless he has come here to shoot me.

MILLY: How romantic!

ROSE: How delightful!

PROCTOR: How out of tune!

MILLY: Perhaps he has only come to ask you to give him back his presents.

ROSE: How horrid of him to bother you when you don't care for him.

BAB: I never said I didn't care for him.

MILLY: Oh!

ROSE: I hear him climbing up the ivy.

MILLY: He is coming to the window.

BAB: If he and Jack meet they will fight. (*To* GIRLS) Leave us.

ROSE *and* MILLY *exeunt.* BAB *hides.* TOM *enters from the window. He is very sad.*

BALLAD.—TOM.

It was the time of thistledown,
 The corn we wandered through;
She plucked the lover's thistledown,
 As maids are wont to do.
She blew upon the thistledown,
 "He loves, he loves me not!"
And from the loyal thistledown,
 "He loves" the answer got.
She did not ask the thistledown

 If her own love were true;
No need to ask the thistledown,
 She thought—as maidens do.
But had she asked the thistledown,
 This answer she'd have got,
"Your false breath stains the thistledown,
 He loves, but you love not."

BAB (*coming down*): Tom! (*They embrace*)

TOM: Then you do love me?

BAB (*kissing him*): Oh no, this is only saying good-bye.

TOM: You fling me over?

BAB: Jack insists on it.

TOM: Have you forgotten that day on the river, when—

BAB: When you kissed my hand? Oh, Tom, but I have been on the river since then with Jack, and he—

TOM: Kissed your hand also?

BAB: No, he did not kiss my—hand. (TOM *takes something wrapped in paper from his pocket*) What is that?

TOM: The glove you gave me. (*Gives it to her*) Give it to Jack. (*Hands her something else*)

BAB: And what is this?

TOM: A hairpin. Give it to Jack. Good-bye!

BAB: Ah, Tom, you will soon forget me.

TOM: I am a man who loves but once, and then for aye.

BAB: You will be heart-broken about me all your life?

TOM: Till the grave close on me.

BAB: Dear Tom, you make me so happy. Now, kiss me passionately for the last time. You must see that it is not my fault. (*He is about to kiss her, then sadly lets her go*)

DUET.—TOM and BAB.

TOM: O eyes that spoke to me of truth,
　　Farewell, deceptive mirror!

BAB: Thus you describe them, yet forsooth,
　　You look into the mirror!

TOM: Sweet mouth that pouted for my kiss,
　　Farewell, sweet lying mouth!

BAB: The words you're using are amiss,
　　Yet sweet you call my mouth!

TOM: O heart that throbbed a tale untrue,
　　Farewell, you falsely beat!

BAB: Although it may not beat for you,
　　The words you say are sweet.

TOM: False one, farewell, I harm you not;
　　To him depart, and scathless;
　　Be mine to bear my dreary lot,
　　　Struck down by woman faithless.

For you, a jilt, my heart has bled,
　　My cup with grief you fill.
Ah, tell me, empty little head,
　　Why 'tis I love you still?
BAB: He loves me still, he loves me true,
　　He worships at my feet.
My heart may never beat for you,
　　And yet your words are sweet.

ENSEMBLE.

TOM.	BAB.
'Tis so; yet joy be thine,	Ah, how can joy be mine,
Though hopeless future mine,	If hopeless fate is thine?
Farewell!	Farewell!

BAB (*aside*): Ah! am I sure that it is Jack whom I love best? And yet, my promise!

JANE ANNIE *steals downstairs.*

BAB: Fly, Tom! It is Jane Annie, the sneak!

TOM *hurries to window where* JANE ANNIE *meets him. The* PROCTOR *comes stealthily out of clock.*

PROCTOR: Name and college!

TOM *jumps through the window*[12], PROCTOR *seizes* JANE ANNIE. BAB *listens unseen.*

JANE A.: Unhand me! I am Jane Annie, the model girl od the school.

PROCTOR: You are Bab, the flirting-girl!

JANE A.: You are mistaken, I—

PROCTOR: Mistaken!—I! Have I not told you that I am a Proctor?

JANE A.: It was Bab who was flirting, and I came to warn you.

PROCTOR: Yes, it was Bab, and you are Bab. (*Seeing* BAB) Girl, what is the name of this chit?

BAB: That is Bab, sir, and my name is Jane Annie.

JANE A.: Oh!

PROCTOR: Exactly! She has assumed your name.

BAB: Oh, Bab, how could you!

PROCTOR: I caught her in the act of eloping with an undergraduate through this window.

Bab: Naughty!

Jane A.: You wicked little wretch! Sir, I am—

Proctor: You are about to be shut up in your bedroom for the night. Which is her room, Jane Annie?

Jane A.: You—

Bab: In the attic there.

Proctor: Come!

Proctor *drags* Jane Annie *upstairs, and pushes her into her room.*

Bab: I hope poor Tom didn't hurt himself, though I believe he went away blaming me. Men are so unreasonable!

Proctor (*coming down*): Well, Jane Annie, why don't you go to bed?

A letter is thrown through the window.

Proctor: A letter! and through the window!

Bab (*aside*): Oh, it is from Jack! We are ruined!

Proctor: It has no address. For whom can it be meant?

Bab: Oh, give it to me, sir?

Proctor: To you, child? Never! It is my duty to open it myself. (*Opens and reads*) "Ten past nine." Ten past nine! I am waiting for you in the garden." Ha! what plot is this that I have unearthed? Who is waiting in the garden, and for whom?

Bab (*aside*): Oh, what shall I do? Ha! Have I not heard that Miss Sims and he were sweethearts? (*To* Proctor) Can you not see?

Proctor: No, I can't; and if I can't, it's perfectly certain that no one else can.

Bab: I know whom the letter is from.

Proctor: From whom, child?

Bab: It is from Miss Sims.

Proctor: From Dinah?

Bab: Precisely.

Proctor: And for whom is she waiting?

Bab: Why, for you, of course. Oh, sir, have pity upon this poor lady's heart.

Proctor: Ha! "Ten past nine!"[13] She means me! Of course it is addressed to me. "Ten past nine, I am waiting for you in the garden." Excuse me, child! (*Exit*)

Bab: Oh, Jack is outside, and I do trust they will not meet. It was my only chance. Now I must put on my hat and coat and slip out to join him.

Exit into bedroom. Jane Annie *comes downstairs.*

JANE A.: That little wretch Bab will find that I am not so easily foiled. Let me see, I need darkness, because I am such a good girl. (*Turns down the lights*) Oh! who is this?

Enter JACK *in a cloak.*

JACK: Bab, come! (*Sees* JANE ANNIE *and runs forward*)

JANE A.: I am not Bab!

JACK: Oh, Lord! the wrong one. (*Takes to his heels, dropping the cloak in his haste*)

JANE A.: What a superior young man! His cloak! (*Puts it on*) In this light she might mistake me for him! (*Swaggers about in military fashion*) Oh, I will lay such a beautiful trap for her! (*Retires to back of stage, and conceals herself by the curtain*)

Enter BAB, *dressed for travelling, and with several packages.*

BAB: Farewell, dear old school—the nicest school in the world to get away from! If I were only sure that I am not making a mistake! They say that there was a girl who eloped from here once, and that she was unhappy, and that her spirit still haunts these rooms. Tom, Tom! shall I take this final step which is to divide us? Oh! what is that?

VOICES IN THE AIR.

Little maiden, pause and ponder,
  Life is cruel, life is dreary.
Little feet, why should you wander
  On to paths so rough and weary?
Ere you snap the final link,
  Little maiden, pause and think!

BAB: Oh, I am so frightened. What shall I do?

JANE ANNIE *comes forward, enveloped in* JACK's *cloak.*

JANE A.: Come!

BAB: Jack, I cannot!

JANE A.: Quick!

BAB: Oh, Jack, be good to me! Do be careful of this packet. It is awfully, awfully important. It is my curling tongs. (*Gives packet*) The carriage is awaiting us, of course. That contains your letters Jack, and these are some little things—and take this bag. And now, darling, carry me down, for I am going to faint!

She falls into JANE ANNIE's *arms, who lets the things fall, seizes her and screams. Ringing of bells, and general alarm.* PRESS STUDENTS *come rushing upstairs.*[14] Miss Sims *enters, all stare at* Jane Annie *holding* Bab, *who seems to have fainted from fright.*

Finale.

Press Students: Madam, do no think us rude in
   On your privacy intrudin';
   We are Students Journalistic,
   Keen on copy, plain or mystic,
   Commonplace or transcendental,
   Psychic, physical, or mental,
   News we'll have, and through you, madam,
   For we'll interview you, madam.
   That's so flat, nought could be flatter,
   Tell us quickly, what's the matter?
   What's the matter? What's the matter?
Girls *run out of their rooms in various stages of deshabille.*[15]
Girls: Madam, when we heard this screaming,
   Scarcely sure if we were dreaming,
   Curiosity controlled us,
   And we came as you behold us,
   Trim or ruffled, tossed or dapper,
   Clad in dressing gown or wrapper,
   We are kneeling to you, madam,
   News to get, and through you, madam.
   Think not this is idle chatter,
   But inform us what's the matter?
   What's the matter? What's the matter?

Ensemble.

Press Students.	Girls.
News we'll have, and	We are kneeling to you,
through you, madam, etc.	madam, etc.

Miss Sims: Jane Annie, what is this?
Bab, what were you doing in her arms?
Bab: Miss Sims, forgive me! I thought she was a gentleman.
Miss Sims: Oh, infamous! To your rooms, all, this instant!
Exeunt Miss Sims, Bab, Jane Annie, *and* Girls.

PRESS STUDENTS (*taking notes eagerly*):
School aristocratic,
The scene most dramatic,
Plot unsystematic,
And very erratic,[16]
Jane Annie ecstatic,
Her victory emphatic,
She won it by stealing
Down from the attic.

Enter PROCTOR *furiously.*

PRESS STUDENTS: We're glad to interview you,
To get a column through you,
And note what you may say.
See now how we will do him,
While we seem to interview him,
In our frank, new-fashioned way.
Are Proctors men of learning?
Do you spend more than you're earning?
And how much do you owe?
Of women do you think much?
On occasion do you drink much?

PROCTOR: Emphatically, no!

PRESS STUDENTS (*writing*): Proctors have no acumen,
And no respect for women.

PROCTOR: Yes, yes! I meant to say!

PRESS STUDENTS (*writing*): In debt and boasts about it.
Love's grog—can't do without it.
Must have it night and day.

PROCTOR: My words you're misconstruing,
That is not interviewing.

PRESS STUDENTS: Yes, this is interviewing,
In the frank, new-fashioned way.

PROCTOR: If you'll suppress this fable,
I'll tell you, if I'm able,
A recent incident.
(*Aside*) Diverting their attention,
I'll draw from my invention
Some singular event.

There was once a man in a seaside town,
    And his name it was—what was it?
I know it wasn't Smith, and I'm sure it wasn't Brown,
    But it was—oh, Lor', what was it?
I very much want to tell you all,
    You'd love to know about it;
But just this point I can't recall,
And as it's immaterial,
    We'd best go on without it.

A widow lived in the same hotel,
    Her name it was—you know it!
He stole to her and whispered—well,
    He whispered, well—Oh, blow it!
I very much want to tell you all,
    You'd love to know about it;
But just this point I can't recall,
And as it's immaterial,
    I'd best go on without it.

But when the lady heard this speech,
    Down to the pier she flew then,
Threw up her arms, and with a screech,
    She—she—Oh, dear! what did she do then?
I very much want to tell you all,
    You'd love to know about it;
But just this point I don't recall,
And as it's most material,
    I can't go on without it.[17]

Enter SIM *and* GREG.

SIM: At last we've got him, sir,

PROCTOR (*not heeding*): Away!

SIM: Him that dangled after her!

PROCTOR: Hurray!

(*addressing* PRESS STUDENTS) To catch an undergraduate I came,

SIM AND GREG (*perplexed*): Of this there's question none,

He is an undergraduate,
    In all respects but one.
That one to mention we forgot,
    It's odd to me and mate,
It's this, that somehow he is not
    An undergraduate!

JACK *steps forward,* CADDIE *holding him.*

ALL: Why, evidently he is not
    An undergraduate!

MILLY (*from balcony*): Oh, sir, take care
        Of one so fair
    Let his complexion
    Plead with you for him!

JACK: An officer I,
        Strolling by,
    Smoking a Henry Clay,[18]
        These men I met,
        They me beset
    In a most unseemly way.
        Of girls they spoke,
        Which spoilt my smoke,
    For the sex I do not care about.
        I've not address't
        Them e'en in jest
    Since '85—or there about.

        They dragged me here,
        By brute force sheer,
    But this doth chiefly jar.
        Your page, I find,
        We left behind
    Smoking my big cigar.
        And therefore I
        Your school defy,
    Oh, I do not stand in awe of you;
        For spoilt have they
        My Henry Clay,
    And I mean to have the law of you.

Exit JACK.

Re-enter GIRLS.

PROCTOR: No I am trepanned and done brown.

PRESS STUDENTS: We hear you, and we've got it down.

Enter MISS SIMS *and* JANE ANNIE.

MISS SIMS (*to* JANE ANNIE): We owe all too you, it appears!
    So what can I do?

GIRLS: Box her ears!

JANE ANNIE: To be good I try hard,

GIRLS: Ain't she meek?

JANE ANNIE: And I ask no reward,

GIRLS: Oh, the sneak!

JANE ANNIE: Yet if I should take
        Something nice,
    They may learn to forsake
        Ways of vice.

PRESS STUDENTS: Stop a moment—"Forsake!"
        "Ways of vice!"

JANE ANNIE: Now the good-conduct prize,

GIRLS: Oh, how mean!

JANE ANNIE: Seems good to my eyes,

GIRLS: Which are green!

JANE ANNIE: So if you agree
        That I'm right,
    Why not give it me
        Well—to-night?

PRESS STUDENTS: Stop a moment—"Agree"
        "To to-night."

MISS SIMS: Dear pupils, see, to my bosom I fold her,
    The prize shall be hers ere she's five minutes older.

Exeunt MISS SIMS, PROCTOR, BULLDOGS, *and* CADDIE.

JANE ANNIE: The girl who's good, demure, correct,
    Cannot preserve her self-respect,
        And mine I would regain.
    So having got the prize to-night,
    To-morrow I, with all my might,
        Will be an imp again!
    Girls, I am naughty from this hour,
        And six long months of wickedness,
    By virtue of my magic power,

Into one day I will compress!
ALL: Jane Annie's naughty from this hour,
    But oh! what is this magic power?
CADDIE *sends* PRESS STUDENTS *away.*[19]

SONG.—JANE ANNIE.

When I was a little piccaninny,
    Only about so high,
I'd a baby's bib and a baby's pinny
    And a queer little gimlet eye.
They couldn't tell why that tiny eye
    Would make them writhe and twist,
They found it so, but how could they know
    That the babe was a hypnotist?

ALL: Now think of that! this tiny brat
    Was a bit of a hypnotist!
JANE ANNIE: And as I grew my power grew too,
    For we were one, you see,
And what I willed the folk would do
    At a wave or a glance from me.
I could "suggest" what pleased me best,
    And still can, when I list,
And Madam Card will find it hard
    To beat this hypnotist!
ALL: Oh, think of it! This little chit
    Is a mighty mesmerist!

DANCE.

Enter MISS SIMS, BULLDOGS, PRESS STUDENTS, *and* CADDIE *in procession.* PAGE *bearing prize.* GIRLS *become demure.*[20]
MISS SIMS: To Jane Annie this prize I present,
    And in it I've writ this inscription—
  "Awarded a hundred per cent.
    For goodness of every description."
        (*Presents prize*)

Miss Sims, Bulldogs, and Page:
    Hail, oh hail to the modest maiden!
        Hail, oh hail to the downcast eyes!
    Now with all our plaudits laden,
        See, she takes the well-earned prize.
           Hail, Jane Annie, hail!
Girls: Hail, oh hail to the scheming maiden,
        Hail, oh hail to the roguish eye!
    Now she stands with honours laden,
        They will know her by-and-bye.
        Hail, Jane Annie, hail!

Ensemble.

Miss Sims, Bulldogs, etc.
    Hail, oh hail to her we honour!
        Hail, oh hail to the blushing cheek!
    Place the laurel wreath upon her,
        See her crowned, and good, and meek!
        Hail, Jane Annie, hail!
Girls: Hail, oh hail to her they honour!
        Hail to her unblushing cheek!
    Place the laurel wreath upon her,
        See her trying to look meek.
        Hail, Jane Annie, hail!

Curtain[21]

Act II

SCENE.—*Golf green near the school. River at back.* BAB, *a prisoner, is walking up and down in* CADDIE's *charge.*

SONG.—CADDIE.

A page-boy am I
That young ladies decry,
Yes, yes, dears, you do, for I hear yer;
But it's little you know
The volcanoes that glow
Inside of this little exterior.
Oh, you wouldn't deride,
Could you step inside
Of this here pocket edition,
And, striking a light,
Perceive that this mite
Is on fire with a grand ambition.[22]

BAB: But at present the buttons he's wearing,
And he's taking me out for an airing.
(*Walks up and down*)

CADDIE: My wife I shall choose
From the class called the Blues,
Whose theory is that they hates men,
Of birthplaces galore
I mean to have more
Than him wot's the eminent statesman.
A peerage I'll take
For my progeny's sake,
To refuse it I think would be shabby,
And I ask poor and rich
To my funeral, which
Will be held in Westminster Abbey.
Oh, you wouldn't deride, etc.

Cries of "Fore! Fore!"

BAB: The girls are playing golf. (*She holds up flag*)

CADDIE: Girls! Poor summer flies!

BAB: Do let me play, Caddie.

CADDIE: It's again the Missus' orders. I'm your jailer, I am, and Miss Sims's words were: "Give the wench a little exercise, but never leave her for a moment, or she will be eloping again; and if she does," said she, "you just pull the big fire bell."

BAB: But why not let me elope, Caddie? See, I go on my knee to you. (*Kneels*)

CADDIE: Get up! Get up!

BAB (*rising*): Cold, relentless! You have never loved!

CADDIE: Have I not? By gum![23]

BAB: You in love. With whom?

CADDIE (*sadly*): It's all over for ever, no more.

BAB: She jilted you?

CADDIE: Well, it came to the same thing, I jilted her.

BAB: Why?

CADDIE: I wanted a bigger one.

BAB: And have you got a bigger one?

CADDIE: I have.

BAB: Whom?

CADDIE (*pointing off stage*): You see that agreeable circumference coming this way?

BAB: Yes.

CADDIE: Well, that's my new one.

BAB: Jane Annie!

BAB *goes sadly up stage. A golf ball lands on green,* CADDIE *pockets it. Enter* JANE ANNIE *with golf club. She looks for her ball.* CADDIE *looks longingly at her and sighs aloud.*

CADDIE: My charmer!

JANE A.: Caddie, did you see my ball?

CADDIE: No, Miss, no balls have come this way.

JANE A.: It is a strange thing that when you are acting as caddie nearly all our balls get lost.

CADDIE: Yes, Miss.

JANE A.: And what is stranger still, those same lost balls are afterwards offered us for sale at your mother's shop in the village.

CADDIE: Ah, it be a puzzling world, Miss.

JANE A. (*putting her hand in his pocket and producing ball*): Now it seems to me that this is my ball.

CADDIE: Extraordinary thing!

JANE A.: How did it get there?

CADDIE: You must have played it into my pocket, Miss.

JANE A.: Fibber! I feel sure that it fell dead just on the edge of the hole—here. (*Puts ball close to hall*)

CADDIE: No, Miss, now that you mention the circumstance, I recollect that I picked it out of the bunker.

JANE A.: Pooh! nonsense!

CADDIE: Is this fair, Miss?

JANE A.: Of course it's fair, so long as nobody sees me. Besides, I'm told they often do it at Felixstowe.[24] Why, even Mr. Balf— (CADDIE *signs silence to her, pointing to private box as if fearful lest they should be overheard. Exit* CADDIE)

BAB: Sneak!

JANE A.: Are you a prisoner, Bab?

BAB: Yes, thanks to you. I shall tell everybody how good you have been. (*Sits down on rug*)

JANE A.: How hateful of you to threaten to take away my character.

BAB: Goody! Goody! Goody!

JANE A. (*sitting down beside* BAB): I'm not really good.

BAB: Yes, you are. You sha'n't sit on my rug. (*Pulls it away*) Why, you promised last night to be dreadfully naughty to-day, so as to make up for your goodness of the past six months, and here you are as shamelessly good as ever.

JANE A.: You do me an injustice. The fun is about to begin. Early this morning I hypnotized our dear mistress, and made her write the most dreadful letters.[25] Just fancy, two of them were invitations to Tom and Jack to come and bring as many male friends with them as they could get together. She has not the least idea of what she has done, of course! Ha! ha!

BAB: But why have you done this?

JANE A.: So that in the confusion Tom and Jack may carry off the girl of their heart.

BAB: But I can only marry one of them.

JANE A.: Yes, but I can marry the other.

BAB: You! But I haven't selected mine yet. That is my difficulty.

JANE A.: No, but I have! That removes your difficulty.

BAB: You toad!

JANE A.: The one I have chosen is Jack.

BAB: Jack! Does he know?

JANE A.: No, I am keeping it a surprise for him.

BAB: I don't believe a word you have said.

JANE A.: You can have my aid if you will promise to take Tom and leave Jack for me. You can't elope without my aid.

BAB: I shall.

JANE A.: You sha'n't!

BAB: Goody! Goody! Goody!

Cries of "Fore! Fore!" are heard, and a ball lands on the green.

JANE A.: The girls.

BAB: Goody! Goody! Goody!

GIRLS *enter in golf costume.* JANE ANNIE, ROSE, MEG, *and* MILLY *are playing a foursome; the others are looking on.* CADDIE *accompanies them as caddie.*[26]

CHORUS OF GIRLS.

> To golf is staid for bashful maid,
>> So our schoolmistress thinks,
> That's why, 'tis said, Queen Mary played
>> On famed St. Andrew's links.

BAB (*holding up her club*):   Niblick!   }
JANE ANNIE (*holding up her club*): Driver!   }
MILLY (*holding up her club*):   Putter!   }
MEG (*holding up her club*):   Brassy!   }

BAB: One up!

JANE ANNIE: Two to play!

ALL: We play the game as that Scotch lassie, Mary, used to play.

This verse is sung with spirit; the second dejectedly.

GIRLS: The game was gay in Mary's day,
>> Her foursomes were not lonely,
> Maybe 'cause they had not to play
>> On greens for ladies only!

BAB (*as before*):   Niblicks!   }
JANE ANNIE (*as before*): Drivers!   }
MILLY (*as before*):   Putters!   }
MEG (*as before*):   Brassies!   }

BAB: One up!

JANE ANNIE: Two to play!

GIRLS: For partners we have only lassies,
　　Which was not Mary's way.
MEG *plays at hole and misses.* CADDIE *chuckles.*
JANE A.: You have flung away the hole.
ROSE *plays at hole and misses.* CADDIE *grins.*
MILLY: Silly! (ROSE *weeps.* MILLY *plays into hole*) Hurrah!
　　Rose and I have done this hole in seventeen![27]
Enter MISS SIMS.
MISS S.: Young ladies, as it is the last day of the term our rules may be
　　a little relaxed.
MILLY: Oh, you dear kind thing!
MISS S.: Except in the case of Bab, who must remain a prisoner all
　　day.
BAB: Oh! Oh! Oh!
MISS S.: So we shall admit some men to to-day's festivities.
ALL: Hurrah! Hurrah! Hurrah!
MISS S.: But not real men.
ROSE: Boys?
MILLY: Oh, I'm going to bed!
MISS S.: No, but half of you may be permitted for this day only to
　　assume the character of men. It will be quite as amusing.
ALL (*dismally*): Oh!
MISS S.: And very much safer.
MILLY (*brightening*): Perhaps this game will provide an answer to a
　　question in deportment which has often puzzled me. It is this.
　　Suppose a gentleman were to put his arm round me, what would
　　be the right thing for me to do?[28]
ROSE: The right thing would be to scream.
MILLY: No. I think the right thing would be not to let on, so that he
　　shouldn't have the satisfaction of knowing that you noticed it.
BAB: I know what I should do if a man put his arm round me —
　　I would stand still.
MISS S.: Shameless! And what would you do, Jane Annie?
JANE A.: I would run to you, madam, for protection.
MISS S.: (*fondling her*): Dear Jane Annie! (*To girls*) Now go.
Exeunt girls. BAB *goes last in charge of* CADDIE.
MISS S.: Now, Jane Annie, dear, there is something strange I want to
　　speak to you about. You remember when you left me in the study
　　this morning?

JANE A.: Yes, Miss Sims.

MISS S.: Well, I must have dropped asleep immediately afterwards, and I had the oddest dreams.

JANE A. (*chuckles, but assumes an air of sympathy as* MISS SIMS *turns towards her*): Dreams, Miss Sims?

MISS S.: Oh, the strangest dreams! I seemed to be writing such a number of letters, but what they were about I cannot imagine.

JANE A.: Of course it was all fancy!

MISS S.: But ten envelopes were missing when I woke.

JANE A.: No!

MISS S.: And my fingers were quite inky. I do hope I have not done anything foolish in my sleep.

JANE A.: I hope not.

MISS S.: Especially just now, while the Proctor is here.

JANE A.: Why specially while he is here?

MISS S.: Ah, Jane Annie, he and I were once—(*Sighs*)[29]

JANE A.: No, were you?

MISS S.: I assure you he often—(*Sighs*)

JANE A.: Did he? Where?

MISS S.: In the conservatory.

JANE A.: Just where they do it to-day.

MISS S.: But, alas! he—(*Sighs*)

JANE A.: How horrid of him.

MISS S.: And so his presence here makes me think of early days when—(*Sighs*)

JANE A.: Naturally.

SONG.—MISS SIMS.

A girl again I seem to be,
    Though I'm an old schoolmistress grey;
Again a boy comes courting me,
    Though he's a hard-faced man to-day.
He calls me little golden-head,
    I feel his kisses on my brow,
I still recall the words he said,
    Though I'm an old schoolmistress now,
Youth dreams of what's to be, I ween,

The future's always far away;
But age must dream of what has been,
    The past is always yesterday.
We meet, but he does not recall

    The golden head, the love-lit eyes;
Our meetings and our partings all
    To him are less than memories.
He twits the old schoolmistress prim,
    Forgetful of his broken vow,
And that she owes it all to him
    That she's an old schoolmistress now.
Youth dreams of what's to be, I ween, etc.

MISS SIMS *is retiring up stage. She returns excitedly.*

MISS S.: There is a party of those impertinent Press Students coming
    sown the river, who look as if they intended to land upon our
    bank.

JANE A. (*in horror*): Oh, surely it cannot be. (*Aside with exultation*) The
    result of letter number one.

MISS S.: Let us go and fetch Caddie to protect us.[30]

Exeunt MISS SIMS *and* JANE ANNIE. *Song of Oarsmen heard in the
distance and coming nearer.*

BARCAROLLE.—PRESS STUDENTS

Where the willows shade the river,
Where the leaning rushes quiver,
Where the water weeds are shining,
Some enfolding, some entwining,
    There we go! Cheerily oh!
        Eight like one we dip and feather!
    Steadily now! Stroke and bow!
        Pulling along and all together!

They land, TOM *among them.*

Enter MISS SIMS, JANE ANNIE, *and* CADDIE.

MISS S. (*shrinking from them*): The wretches! (*To* CADDIE) Order them
    to go at once, Caddie.

CADDIE (*turning up his sleeves fiercely*): Come now, you had best go
    quietly.

Tom: What does this sprat mean?

Caddie: Sprat! Summer flies! Now, look here, are you going quietly, or must I chuck the blooming lot of you into the river?

Tom: There is some mistake, madam—we came here by invitation.

Caddie: Look here, I know that game.

Miss S.: Impossible! By whose invitation?

Tom (*producing letter*): By yours—here is your letter. (*Hands it to her*)

Jane A. (*aside*): Exquisite!

Miss S. (*reading*): "Dear Mr. Tom, as I have seen you in the neighbourhood of my school more than once, I venture to ask whether you will do me the honour of attending a garden party which I am giving to my girls this afternoon. I want to show them a little life. Please bring a few of those pleasant Press Students, and be sure to come in cap and gown. It will be a free and easy affair. My girls join me in sending love, and I am yours sincerely, Dinah Sims." Oh!

Caddie (*shocked*): Well, of all the—! The old girl is coming out of her hegg at last. (*Exit*)

Miss S.: Oh, Jane Annie, is it not dreadful? I could not have written such a letter.

Jane A.: Well, it is certainly in your writing.

Tom (*aside*): Now to look for Bab. (*Exit*)

Enter Caddie.

Caddie: If you please, ma'am, the man has come with the Scotch whisky.

Miss S.: Whisky! there is some mistake. I never ordered any.

Caddie: Why, ma'am, you sent me this morning with a letter to the wine-merchant, ordering two dozen of whisky and one dozen of soda.

Miss S.: Oh, this is too much!

Caddie: That's what I thought, ma'am, too much whisky and not enough soda.

Exit Miss Sims.

1st Stud.: We were invited—and we'll stay.

All: Certainly. (*Sit down in a determined manner*)

Caddie (*to* Jane Annie): See here, Miss, I have knocked about a bit in my time, and it strikes me that you have been doing something fishy.

Jane A.: Go away!

CADDIE: What's more, I have the responsibility of this here seminary on my shoulders, and I'll find out what you've been up to, and expose you, if you don't—

JANE A.: Don't what?

CADDIE: If you don't chuck us a kiss.

JANE A.: There! (*Slaps his face*)

CADDIE (*puzzled*): See here now, is that flirting, or ain't it?

JANE A.: It "ain't."

CADDIE: Then drop it—and give us a kiss.

JANE A.: Sha'n't!

CADDIE: This is the last time of asking. You'll never have such a chance again.

JANE A.: There! (*Slaps him*)

CADDIE: Summer flies! Now for revenge. (*Exit*)

JANE A.: It's all very well to laugh, but he is quite capable of doing what he threatens, and so I—I think I had better give him a kiss. (*Exit after* CADDIE)

Cries of "Fore!" and two golf balls land on the putting green. The balls are followed by some of the GIRLS, *who look self-consciously at the* STUDENTS. *The* STUDENTS *look very sheepish.*

1ST STUD.: Speak to them, Christopherson.

2ND STUD.: Say something nice, Tippy.

3RD STUD.: I can't think of anything nice to say.

2ND STUD.: Well, then, let us look nice. (*All simper*)

MILLY: Are you men?

STUDENTS. Eh, what? We are. Oh, yes, certainly, certainly.

MILLY: So are we.

1ST STUD.: Eh?

MILLY: You see, Miss Sims, our mistress, has invented a new game for us. Half of our number are to be men for to-day, and to entertain the other half.

2ND STUD.: But where's the other half?

MILLY: Oh, that was the difficulty. You see, we all wanted to be men, so there is no other half.

2ND STUD.: You're all men, then?

MILLY: Yes, and we don't know what to do for girls.

3RD STUD.: A gentlemen will do anything to oblige a lady, will not he, friends?

ALL: Certainly.

3RD STUD.: Then, let us be girls.

MILLY: Delightful, and we'll be students.

The GIRLS *put on the caps and gowns of the* STUDENTS, *and swagger about in a manly way. The* STUDENTS *look shy and mincing.*

MILLY (*to* 1ST STUDENT): Ah, ah, ah! What are these things you are carrying?

1ST STUD. (*consciously*): Ah, ah, ha! Kodaks.

MILLY: Ah—ah—no!

1ST STUD.: Ah—ah—yes! (*They giggle and* MILLY *runs to* ROSE)

MILLY: Rose, you can't guess how I have been flirting with that dark one.

1ST STUD. (*to* 2ND STUDENT): I say, old man, I have been going the pace with little blue eyes.

ROSE: I haven't felt so wicked since I ate twelve penny tarts at a sitting.[31]

2ND STUD. (*to* 1ST STUDENT): He, he, he! my one asked me what time it was. Oh, what a lark!

MILLY (*hysterically, swaggering*): Glass of beer, waiter—have a weed? How are you, old man?—Glass of beer—have a weed?—how are you, old man? Have a weed—glass of beer. Oh, Jenny, isn't it splendid? Glass of beer—have a weed?—

MAUD: Control yourself, dear.

MILLY: I can't! This cloak has gone to my head. Glass of beer—

PROCTOR *rushes in accompanied by* BULLDOGS. *He cries "Name and College!" The* STUDENTS *rush off, the* GIRLS *all turn their backs.*

PROCTOR: Now, I've got you. There's no mistake this time, at any rate. (*Takes out note-book*) Name and college, sir?

GIRLS: Smith of Olds, Jones of New, Brown of New, etc.

PROCTOR (*pompously*): Now, Gentlemen of the Press, I have got you. For weeks you have followed me with your impertinent note-books and Kodaks. I shall gate the lot of you!

They all rush off laughing, having taken off their caps, and reveal themselves as girls.

PROCTOR: There now! I knew they were girls all the time.

SIM: Of course, if you say so that is sufficient.

GREG: Fudge!

PROCTOR: Hum! Well, perhaps I did make a mistake this time.

SIM: No, no.

PROCTOR: And that no one may say that there is one law for the humble undergraduate and another for the great Proctor, I hereby fine myself one shilling.

SIM: There's a sense of justice, Greg!

PROCTOR: And I shall pay it after my usual fashion.

SIM AND GREG: Don't!

PROCTOR: Namely by proxy. Come, my men, a sixpence each.

They pay reluctantly.

GREG: Da—da—da—

SIM: Greg, forbear.

GREG: It seems to me that we do nine-tenths of the work and you get nine-tenths of the pay.

SIM: Oh, this dashed independence!

PROCTOR: Well, you can't expect to get both the work and the pay. They never go together, even in our Government offices.

GREG: Then they should.

SIM: Greg, Greg! you are flying in the face of the law of England.

GREG. I say it's a da—da—da—

SIM: Greg!

PROCTOR: This discussion is getting hot. Perhaps I had better clear the air with a song, the little thing that you two composed.

GREG: But we composed it about ourselves.

PROCTOR: It suits me better than you. But I am willing to pay for it.

SIM. There's generosity.

PROCTOR: I will pay for it by prox—

SIM AND GREG: You can have it for nothing.

PROCTOR: Thank you,

The music for song is started, PROCTOR *hesitates, yawns.*

PROCTOR: No, it is too great a fag. You shall sing it for me instead.

GREG: At last!

SIM: Always considerate!

PROCTOR: But remember, you are to sing it about me—not about yourselves.

GREG: Da—

SIM: Hush!

TRIO.—BULLDOGS and PROCTOR.

When I was a—when he was a little child
    Only two or three,
All the household went quite wild
    Out of love for—he.

Cooks and housemaids came to kiss,
    Crowding for their duty,
And the reason for all of this,
    Was our—my—his too—too—too—
    His too fatal beauty.

When I was a—when he was a little man,
    Only just of age,
Off to London then he ran,
    And became the rage.
High and low they loved us so—him so,
    And claimed him for their booty;
And the reason well I know,
Was our—was my—was his too—too—too—
    His too—too fatal beauty.

DANCE.

PROCTOR *takes the applause meant for* BULLDOGS *and exit.*
SIM: You can say it now, Greg.
GREG: —!
BULLDOGS *exeunt arm in arm, R.*
Enter OFFICERS *and* JACK.

MILITARY CHORUS.—JACK and OFFICERS.

OFFICERS: We are conscious that we slightly condescend,
JACK: Right turn!
OFFICERS: But we couldn't go and disoblige a friend,
JACK: Left turn!
OFFICERS: Yet it's infra dig, you see,
    For such warriors as we
      To come out to cakes and tea
        At a school.
JACK: Stand at ease!
JACK: Now a midnight oyster supper would be nice,
OFFICERS: Very nice!
JACK: Or anything with just a touch of vice;
OFFICERS: Just a spice

JACK: But coming fresh, you know,
 From slaughtering the foe,
 It's just a trifle slow
  At a school!
OFFICERS: Mark time
OFFICERS: Now a midnight oyster supper would be nice,
JACK: Right turn!
OFFICERS: Or anything with just a touch of vice;
JACK: Left turn!
OFFICERS: But coming fresh, you know,
 From slaughtering the foe,
 It's just a trifle slow
  At a school!
JACK: Dress line!
JACK: Yet from the invitation it is clear,
OFFICERS: Quite clear!
JACK: There are maids whose leisure moments we may cheer;
OFFICERS: Hear! Hear!
JACK: So as a soldier brave
 Is ever beauty's slave,
 We had a wash and shave,
  And we've come!
OFFICERS: Yet from the invitation it is clear,
JACK: Left turn!
OFFICERS: There are maids whose leisure moments we may cheer;
JACK: Right turn!
OFFICERS: So as a soldier brave
 Is ever beauty's slave,
 We had a wash and shave,
  And we've come!
JACK: Stand at ease!
Enter MISS SIMS *and* JANE ANNIE.
MISS S.: How dare you come here!
JACK: We come by invitation, madam. Haw!
MISS S.: Whose invitation?
JACK: Yours.
MISS S.: I invite you here! You are mad!
JACK: We had a letter from you.[32]
MISS S. (*distracted*): Oh, these letters! (*Talks aside to* JANE ANNIE)

JACK (*to* 1ST OFFICER): Never mind her. I want you all to flirt
    outrageously with the other girls, and while Miss Sims is trying
    to stop you I shall bolt with Bab. Do you think you could do that,
    old man? (OFFICER *Pulls his moustache confidently*) Ask the others.
    (1ST OFFICER *goes to other* OFFICERS, *who repeat business*)

Enter CADDIE.

CADDIE: Please, ma'am, the brass band is here.

MISS S.: Brass band!

CADDIE: Yes, ma'am, they say they had a letter from you. And the
    man has come with the bull-pups.[33]

MISS S.: Oh, I am going mad!

CADDIE: Yes, ma'am.

MISS S.: Let us go and lock the gates. (*Exit excitedly*)

JANE A. (*to* CADDIE): Do let me kiss you, Caddie!

CADDIE: Too late! Revenge!

JANE A.: But you wanted me to do it five minutes ago.

CADDIE: I was a boy then. (*Exit*)

Enter some of the GIRLS *from a boat.*

JACK (*to* JANE ANNIE): Do you know where my Bab is?

JANE A.: Bother Bab!

JACK: Eh?

JANE A.: I had such a nice dream about you, last night.

JACK: No, had you? Haw!

JANE A.: Yes, I dreamt that you were to elope with me instead of with
    Bab.

JACK: Not if I know it.

JANE A.: Perhaps you won't know it at this time—but you'll know it
    afterwards.

JACK (*aside*): I dislike this girl very much.

JANE A. (*to* GIRLS *who are flirting with* OFFICERS): I have been left in
    charge to see that you all behave yourselves.

ROSE: Oh!

JANE A.: You and I, Jack, will set them an example.

CONCERTED PIECE.—
JANE ANNIE, JACK, GIRLS, OFFICERS, AND STUDENTS.

JANE ANNIE: You and I, dear Jack, will show
    A most excellent example.

JACK: Scarce can they in virtue grow,
    If they take me for their sample.
JANE ANNIE: If you list to my advice,
    Keep young men at a safe distance.
She draws JACK's *arm round her waist.*
JACK: This is strange, and yet it's nice,
    I shall offer no resistance.

ENSEMBLE.

GIRLS.	OFFICERS.
In accord with her advice,	This is strange, and yet it's nice,
We shall keep you at a distance.	We shall offer no resistance.

Drawing OFFICERS' *arms round.*
ALL: We/They have learned her/my precept pat,
    We/They mustn't do that! We/They mustn't do that!
    And so, of course, the sequence is,
    We/They mustn't do this! We/They mustn't do this!
JANE ANNIE: You and I will also show
    A correct and sober bearing.
JACK: Though her words are cold as snow,
    Yet her glance is most ensnaring.
JANE ANNIE: If you list to my advice,
    You will never start off dancing.
        (*Dancing several steps*)
JACK: Though she's most severe on vice,
    Yet her ways are most entrancing.

ENSEMBLE.

GIRLS.	OFFICERS.
In accord with her advice,	Though she's very hard on vice,
We shall never start off dancing.	Yet her ways are most entrancing.

All dance.
ALL: We/They have learned her/my precept pat, etc.
Enter STUDENTS *and other* GIRLS.
OFFICERS: What's the meaning of all this?
    Who are these who disconcert us?
STUDENTS: Maidens this is much amiss,

Surely you would not desert us?

Officers: Beardless boys, you'd better go,
   Your time hasn't come, we vow.

Students: Aged men, you're most de trop,
   Your time was, it's over now.

Chorus.

Officers: Maidens, maidens, can you hesitate?

Girls: Hey, dear, we haven't got an answer!

Officers: Maidens, maidens, your reply we wait.

Girls: Hey, dear, the Student or the Lancer!

Students: Maidens, we are fresh from college,
      Smile upon us, we implore you!
   Think of all the varied knowledge
      In these heads which bow before you.
               (*All bow*)

Officers: Maidens, with our martial bearing
      And our spurs, we ought to suit you;
   Think of all the deeds of daring
      Done with hands which now salute you.
               (*All salute*)

Students: Maidens, maidens, can you hesitate?

Girls: Hey, dear, the Student or the Lancer!

Officers: Maidens, maidens, your reply we wait.

Girls: Hey, dear, this must be our answer!

Girls *cross over to* Students.

Students: Maidens, you are wise in turning
      Thus to those who most impress you;
   You shall list to words of learning
      From these lips which now caress you.
               (*Kiss them*)

Officers: Maidens, all their vows are idle.
      Here to you our hands we proffer;
   Fresh from sword-hilt and from bridle,
      Here they are, and all on offer.
               (*Offer their hands*)

Students: Maidens, maidens, do not hesitate.

Girls: Hey, dear, we gave you both our answer!

OFFICERS: Maidens, maidens, what shall be our fate.

GIRLS: Hey, dear, we much prefer the Lancer!

GIRLS *cross over and join* OFFICERS. *Music continues softly through following dialogue.*

A STUD.: But this is absurd! We are all very distinguished men, or shall be some day. And then we are journalists, and can describe your dresses in the papers.

GIRLS: Oh! (*Cross over to* STUDENTS)

JACK: But we shave twice a day.

A STUD.: Why, there is not of us who could not read Theocritus in the original.

JACK: But we are to give a dance next week.

MILLY: Oh, you dear things, how nice of you! (*Cross to* OFFICERS)

Dance. All exeunt except JACK.

JACK: And now to find Bab.

Enter TOM.

TOM: I can't see my Bab anywhere. (*Sees* JACK) Hullo!

JACK: That fellow here!

TOM (*shortly*): How are you?

JACK (*shortly*): H'are you?

TOM (*after a pause*): Very warm day.

JACK: Cold.

TOM: Cad!

JACK: What do you want here?

TOM: Private business.

JACK: Let us be plain with one another. How could you, a beggarly Press Student, support a wife?

TOM: How could you, a beggarly lieutenant?

JACK: But I am also a novelist—at least I've—I've bought a pound of sermon paper. Haw!

TOM: Well, I am also a dramatist. Why, I have a completed play in my pocket.

JACK: And a very good place for it too. Haw!

TOM: What is more, it has a strong literary flavour.

JACK: Don't be afraid of that. They'll knock it out in rehearsal. Haw!

TOM: Nonsense. It's most original also.

JACK: That'll damn it.

TOM: Originality damn a play! Why?

JACK: Because ours are a healthy-minded public, sir, and they won't stand it. Haw!

TOM: It's an Ibsenite play.

JACK: Then why not produce it at the Independent Theatre?

TOM: I did.

JACK: Well?

TOM: And it promised to be a great success; but, unfortunately, just when the leading man has to say, "What a noble apartment is this," the nail came out and the apartment fell into the fireplace.[34]

Enter CADDIE *and* BAB. *They walk back and forwards as before.*

JACK (*amazed*): Bab!

BAB: Oh, Jack! Oh, Tom!

CADDIE: Silence!

JACK: What does this mean?

BAB: I am a prisoner, he is giving me an airing.

CADDIE: Silence!

JACK (*drawing his sword*): Promise not to interfere, or I shall run you through, by the bones of my ancestors!

CADDIE (*aiming a catapult at him*): Advance another step and you are a dead man, so help my bob![35]

JACK *is discomfited, but* TOM *seizes* CADDIE *from behind, and they get him to the ground.*

JACK: Promise!

CADDIE: I gives in! You have my word of honour! It's your hole. (*Mimicking* JACK) Haw! (*Exit* CADDIE *followed by* TOM)[36]

JACK: My precious! The gates are locked, but we can cross the river.

BAB: I have been thinking that—I'm not sure whether it is you or Tom I prefer.

JACK: That is awkward.

BAB: Before I decide I want to ask you both two questions.

JACK: What are they?

BAB: First, why did my heart beat so violently last night?

JACK: It was because—because I am so worthy of its love. Haw!

BAB (*aside*): H'm! Vanity!

JACK (*aside*): Good answer I think. Hope I shall get round her wealthy papa as easily.

BAB: Second, will you still love me when I am old and wrinkled?

JACK (*aside*): I question it. (*Aloud*) Don't talk of anything so unpleasant, dear. Let us try to think that we shall always be young and handsome.

BAB (*aside*): I don't like that answer.

JACK (*aside*): I flatter myself I got out of that bunker very neatly.

TOM *re-enters.*

BAB: Now go, while I ask Tom.

JACK (*aside*): She's mine! Haw! Haw! (*Exit*)

DUET.—BAB AND TOM.

BAB: Last night when we were forced to part
   I heard a pit-a-pat
  Upon the window of my heart—
   Tom, tell me what was that?
    Oh, tell me true,
     For I'm a little maid,
     Of all the world afraid.

TOM: 'Twas my heart which would entrance win,
   'Twas 'neath the window hiding,
  You raised the sash, and said "Come in,"
   And there it's now residing.

BAB: Tom, will your love grow cold to me
   When silvered is my hair?
  Or do you make believe that we
   Shall aye be young and fair?
    Oh, tell me true,
     For I'm a little maid,
     Of all the world afraid.

TOM: Eternal youth's for no one here,
   That secret's to discover;
  But when you're old and grey, my dear,
   I still will be your lover.

BOTH: I've/He's told her/me true
   This little maid
   No longer is afraid.
  Come joy or strife,
   Come weal or woe,

> Sunshine or stormy weather,
> As man and wife
> We'll face the foe,
> And face him thus together.

Tom: Oh, Bab—you will be my wife?

Bab: Yes, if you want me very, very much, Tom.[37]

Enter Bulldogs *and* Proctor *softly R.* Tom *sees them and flies L.* Bulldogs *rush after him and exeunt.*

Bab: Oh! (*Jumps into* Proctor's *arms*) Saved!

Proctor: Caught, you mean.

Bab: No, saved.

Proctor: Eh, what? I don't understand.

Bab: I was only going with him because he promised to take me to you.

Proctor: To me?

Bab: Oh, I feel so safe now that I have reached you—you are so solid and satisfying, like a great plum pudding, you know.

Proctor: You mean well, my child, I have no doubt; but you have an unfortunate way of expressing yourself. (*He puts arm round her.* Tom *rushes across stage and exit. He is followed by* Bulldogs. *They stop when they see* Proctor *and* Bab)

Greg: Hullo!

Sim: Ahem!

Proctor: What do you mean?

Sim: Beg pardon, but your arm you know—eh?

Proctor (*fiercely*): What about my arm?

Greg: It is round—don't you see?

Proctor: I do not.

Greg: Allow me. (*Takes* Proctor's *arm off* Bab)

Proctor: Oh, thanks!

Bab: Oh, there is Miss Sims! Save me, Mr. Proctor!

Proctor: In here, quick! (*Pushes* Bab *into arbour*) She is a nice girl. (*To* Bulldogs) Remember, you have not seen any girl here, if you are asked.

Greg: Not here! Why, she is in the arbour.

Proctor: There is no one in the arbour. What you see is—is an optical illusion. Furthermore, my orders to you are that you see no one in the arbour for the next half-hour, do you hear?

Sim: We—we hear.

PROCTOR (*aside*): In half an hour I am sure I can convince Bab of the
error of her ways. (*Aloud*) And stop, if any one inquires for me,
I am—I am—gathering flowers by the river's brim. Do you—do
you—

GREG: Twig?

PROCTOR: Yes, twig?

SIM AND GREG: We twig.

PROCTOR: Good. (*Goes to* BAB)

GREG: Now, Sim, do you give him up?

SIM (*after a struggle*): No!

Exeunt L., expostulating with each other. BAB. *I knew that you would
save me.*

PROCTOR: Yes, but you must me a good girl in future. You know it's
best in the long run.

BAB: Oh, how beautifully you talk!

PROCTOR: To be happy you must be good.

BAB: Yes, but to be awfully, dreadfully, excruciatingly happy, you must
be naughty. But I am sure I should be good if Miss Sims would
talk to me as you have done.

PROCTOR: Really! Do you mind my calling you Baby?

BAB: Not at all. May I call you Little One?

PROCTOR: Certainly. Do you know I feel a strange something creeping
over me!

BAB: So do I.

PROCTOR: I like it!

BAB: So do I.

PROCTOR: Yum yum!

BAB: So do I.

DUET.—BAB and PROCTOR.

PROCTOR: I'm a man of erudition,
     And a scorner of frivolities,
  With loftiest ambition,
     And most domineering qualities.
  The rowdiest grow meeker
     When I fix them with this eye;
  But I feel I'm growing weaker,
     And I don't know why—

No I don't—not I.
I'm growing quite gelatinous, and can't guess why.

BAB: I'm just a little girlie,
  Who still am in my teens, you know.
For love it's much too early,
  And I can't guess what it means, you know.
But since I saw that simper,
  And the twinkle of that eye,
I feel I'm growing limper,
  And I can't guess why—
    No I can't—not I.
I'm growing quite invertebrate, and can't tell why.

PROCTOR: I've a will that's adamantine,
  And my nerve is quite unshakable,
My strength is elephantine,
  And my spirit is unbreakable,
I cow the flippant cabby,
  I can make the coster cry,
Yet I feel I'm growing flabby,
  And I can't tell why—
    No I can't—not I.
I'm growing quite blanc-mangeical, and can't tell why.

BAB: I'm just a little dolly,
  With an uneventful history,
They tell me love is jolly
  But to me it's still a mystery.
I love my playthings dearly,
  And my dolls and apple pie,
But I'm feeling, oh, so queerly,
  And I can't tell why—
    No I can't—not I.
I'm growing quite gutta-perchical, and can't tell why.

PROCTOR: I fancy that this weakness
  May seem to you undignified.
BAB: Ah me, these words of meekness,
  Now tell me what they signified?
BOTH: Your love can hide no longer,
  It beckons from your eye;
We're unquestionably stronger,

And we both know why.

Do you? So do I.

We are feeling dry-champagnified,

And both know why.

BAB: Oh, how nice-looking you are! You would look so pretty with this round your neck. (*Puts her long boa round*) Now, it should come across your chest like that. (PROCTOR *smiles indulgently*) Then round like this, and fasten so. (*Ties it behind the chair and fastens it. Then laughs and claps her hands*)

PROCTOR (*struggling to rise*): What is this? What do you mean?

BAB: Oh, he mustn't make a noise. (*Puts a handkerchief round his mouth. PROCTOR glares horribly and frowns*) Ha! ha! ha! (*Goes up stage calling "Tom!" PROCTOR gurgles. The BULLDOGS enter and stand one on each side of the arbour*)

GREG: There is no one in the arbour, Sim.

SIM: N—No. (PROCTOR *gurgles*) I thought—

GREG: So did I. But it's only an optical illusion, Sim.

SIM: So it is, Greg. I wonder where the Proctor is?

GREG: He is gathering flowers by the river's brim.

BULLDOGS *close arbour and retire.*

Enter TOM.

TOM: Now, darling, are you ready?

BAB: My own! (*They embrace*)

Enter JACK *followed by* JANE ANNIE.

JACK (*aside*): I am sure she will choose me. Eh—ah—ho — what's this?

BAB: Don't you see?

JACK: I wish I didn't. Haw!

BAB: Jane Annie, you promised to help me if I took Tom.

JANE A.: And I shall.

JACK (*aside*): That unpleasant girl again.

TOM: But what can you do?

JANE A.: One of the letters I made Miss Sims write was to the livery stables, requesting that a carriage should be sent to the other side of the river at two o'clock today. It is there now.

TOM: Are you sure?

JANE A.: Listen! (*She whistles—an answering whistle is heard*) See, there it is! (*A carriage is seen driving up*)

BAB: Let us cross at once.

JANE ANNIE *signs to carriage to go on, and it goes out of sight.*

CADDIE (*entering*): You can't get away. Ho! ho!

BAB: Why not?

CADDIE: Because I've locked the boat-house and hidden the key.

JACK: Good boy!

CADDIE: That's a stimie for you.

TOM: Quick, the key!

CADDIE: Sha'n't!

BAB: What's to be done?

JANE A.: Leave him to me. (*Hypnotizes* CADDIE) Now give me the key.

CADDIE *begins to undress.*

JACK: What is he doing?

TOM: The key must be concealed about his person.

BAB: This is becoming improper.

TOM: Wait a moment. (*To* CADDIE) Caddie, where is the key?

CADDIE *whispers to him.* TOM *whistles and whispers to* JACK, *who rubs his hands gleefully*

BAB: Tom, do something with him at once!

TOM (*primly*): If Caddie will retire with me to some secluded spot for a few moments I shall return with the key.

Exeunt TOM *and* CADDIE.

BAB: Good-bye, Jane Annie, dear.

JANE A.: But I am coming with you.

BAB: You?

JANE A.: Yes, and so is Jack.

JACK: Not I.

JANE A.: Silly boy, yes, you are. Tom is eloping with Bab, and you are eloping with me.

JACK: I'll see you far enough first.

JANE A.: Isn't he shy?

TOM (*entering*): The key!

BAB: Jane Annie proposes that she and Jack should come with us.

TOM: But the carriage will seat only two.

JANE A.: Well, that won't matter.

BAB: Won't it? (JANE ANNIE *chuckles*) Oh Tom! Jane Annie and I see no difficulty.

TIM: How? (*He and* JACK *chuckle*) Do you agree?

JACK: If you will exchange girls. Haw!

TOM: Never!

BAB: Come, Tom.

JANE A.: Come, Jack, and make it a foursome.

JACK: This girl terrifies me. I'll bolt. (*Exit*)

JANE A.: Come back. (*To* TOM) Don't go without us. (*Exit*)

BAB: Now let us fly at once.

TOM: Would it not be a little shabby?

BAB: Not in the least.

Bell begins to toll.

BAB: We are betrayed.

TOM: It is Jack—the villain—I see him.

BAB: Quick, we have time yet.

They are going to the boat-house. CADDIE *appears.*

CADDIE: Back! (*They run L. Enter* MISS SIMS, L.)

MISS S.: Back! (*They run R. Enter* JACK, R.)

JACK: Back!

The GIRLS, STUDENTS, *and* OFFICERS *rush on.*

MISS S.: Seize them! (JACK *seizes* TOM, *and* CADDIE *seizes* BAB)

TOM: Infamous!

JANE A.: It isn't his hole yet! (*Hypnotizes* MISS SIMS)

BAB: She is hypnotized!

ALL: Oh, wonderful!

JANE A.: Now, see what I shall make her do.

SEXTET.—JANE ANNIE, MISS SIMS, BAB, PROCTOR,
JACK, and TOM.

JANE ANNIE: You're now a sentimental maid,
    The little god caressing,
  Dear mistress, we can't have it said
    We went without your blessing.

JANE ANNIE, BAB, TOM, *and* JACK *kneel,* JANE ANNIE *forcing* JACK *to do so.*

QUARTET: We're kneeling, sentimental maid,
  A-waiting for your blessing.

ALL: We hear with wonder what they've said,
  But will she give her blessing?

MISS S.: I'm now a sentimental thing,
    And hear with pride and joy,
  The news, which you two darlings bring,
    That each has found a boy.

J.M. BARRIE AND SIR ARTHUR CONAN DOYLE

Elope, my dears? Why, certainly,
 'Tis every schoolgirl's mission,
And tell your parents you had my
 Approval and permission.
ALL: Their conduct's praised, we are amazed,
 Miss Sims doth sympathize.
Now let us sing of this wonderful thing,
 With a hyp-hyp-hypnotize!

PROCTOR *rushes in from arbour with seat tied to him.*
PROCTOR: Stop! Though this Bab has used me ill—
BAB: Oh, how I wish I'd shot him!
PROCTOR: My triumph's coming now—
TOM: Stand still!
STUDENTS *get Kodaks ready.*
PROCTOR: Eh, what?
TOM: All ready? (*Click*) Got him.
JANE ANNIE *hypnotizes* PROCTOR.
JANE ANNIE: You're now a somewhat soft old boy,
 Whate'er the consequences,
Be yours the privilege and joy
 To pay all our expenses.
QUARTET: We're kneeling, somewhat soft old boy,
 Requesting our expenses.
ALL: Now is he such a soft old boy
 That he'll pay their expenses?
PROCTOR: I'm now a very soft old boy, (*Hear, hear*)
 Elopements are my passion,
So with delight without alloy
 I'll help you in this fashion.
It's sometimes said that gold's a curse. (*No, no!*)
 And love the only candy,
But, Tom, to you I give my purse—
 I think you'll find it handy. (*Cheers*)
ALL: Tho' love is honey, they've taken the money,
 And he doth sympathize;
With this strange thing, his college will ring,
 With a hyp-hyp-hypnotize!
Dance. TOM *and* BAB *go in boat.*
JANE A. (*to* MISS SIMS): Now go and be a tea-pot. (*To* PROCTOR)

And you are an escape of gas.

JACK: I wish I was well out of this.

JANE A.: Come, Jack.

JACK: I refuse.

JANE A. (*hypnotizes him*): You are my lover!

JACK: Darling! (*He goes to boat*)

JANE A.: I took that whole in two!

JANE ANNIE *joins the others in boat. All wave handkerchiefs.*

PROCTOR: Hyp-hyp-hyp-

CHORUS: -notize!

MISS S.: Another!

CHORUS: Hyp-hyp-hypnotize!

PROCTOR: One more!

CHORUS: Hyp-hyp-hypnotize!

JANE A. (*from boat*): Now, old things, wake up!

Exit boat. MISS SIMS *and* PROCTOR *wake up.*

BULLDOGS *enter excitedly.*

MISS S.: What is this?

PROCTOR: Who is in that boat?

MILLY: It's Bab and Jane Annie going away to be married.

MISS S.: What?

CADDIE (*rushing on*): I can't stand it! I can't stand it! Man and boy I've been here eighteen months, and I never thought to see such goings on as this. I gives a month's warning from to-day.

The carriage is seen crossing.

MILLY: The carriage! There they go!

FINALE.

MILLY: The moral of this story is—[38]

GIRLS: You mustn't do this, you mustn't do this;

MILLY: Or to express it still more pat—

GIRLS: You mustn't do that, you mustn't do that.

MISS SIMS: You've learned it now without a hitch—

MEN: We mustn't do what, we mustn't do which?

MISS SIMS: Well, you have learned it, have you not?

MEN: We mustn't do which, we mustn't do what?

PROCTOR: The moral I will now explain,

  Just wait while I expound it;

It teaches that we ne'er again
    Should try to—oh, confound it!
I very much want to tell you all—
    You'd like to hear about it—
But just this point I can't recall,
So, though it's most material,
    You'd best go home without it.
ALL: You'd best go home without it.[39]

Appendix

Notes By Caddie

Act I

[1] When the collaborators came to the school to hear about the Good Conduct Prize scandal, it was me as showed them round, and they asked me to do important notes on the margin. My first important note is that I am a principal, which is more than a lot of the girls are. Yah!—Caddie.

[2] I took it to my bedroom, which was beneath the kitchen table, and it went on striking all night, and I couldn't get no sleep till I turned it out into the garden.

[3] If I had been Bab I would have had the paper out in a jiffy.

[4] They used to put nettles in Jane Annie's bed.

[5] Jane Annie had never got a prize in her life, and she knew this was her only chance.

[6] I once caught Bab slipping a rose into Jack's hand when on the way to church, and she wickedly gave me sixpence not to tell.

[7] Miss Sims was the kind of mistress as is always making you turn out your pockets.

[8] If I had been there I would have seen through Bab, but I was in the kitchen at the time cleaning the knives.

[9] She knew I had took away the works. She's always prying about. Cook wants to write an important note here, but I won't let her, for she is not even in the chorus. One of the collaborators (*the good one*) was willing to give her a line, but the other wouldn't hear of it.

[10] Sim was done by one of the collaborators and Greg by the other one, and that is why they always clashed.

[11] The girls' boots was a regular study. Bab was always stealing the laces out of the other boots to put into her own. Polly Littlejohn was the carelessest girl, and used bits of string for laces. Jenny's heels were in the middle of her boots, to give her a small foot. Jane Annie's size was

threes, and I could put her shoes into Mary Finch's shoes, and Mary Finch's into Kate Arnold's. This used to rile Kate Arnold.

[12] Tom fell into the water-butt, and I saw him from the kitchen window, and helped him out for twopence.

[13] His nickname now is "Ten Past Nine," and they do say he wakes up at that hour every morning, and puts his watch on a bit.

[14] The Press Students had been following the Proctor to get copy out of him; and that is how they were near enough to hear Jane Annie screaming. They couldn't have got in if the Proctor had not forgotten to shut the door.

[15] Rubbidge! They put on their Sunday dressing jackets so to look their best. That was why the Press Students were in before them.

[16] Greg and Sim has a bet that the critics will quote the third and fourth line here, and say that they apply to the opera.

[17] Though they never got the story out of him, they drew a picture of him dancing, and he saw it in a newspaper next day.

[18] It was no more a Henry Clay than I am. It was the kind that you get at seven for a shilling.

[19] I let them come back afterwards because they promised to put my portrait in the papers, but they broke their word.

[20] The reason Miss Sims was such a long time away was that she was rubbing the price off the book with a bit of bread.

[21] The collaborators bring the curtain down here, but a lot took place after that; and what with the Press Students wanting to interview Jane Annie, and the girls cackling about whether Jane Annie would really misbehave next day, and the Proctor going about muttering "Ten past nine," I didn't get to bed till nearly midnight.

Act II

[22] Mine is a very difficult part, and what I want the critics to say about it is that it would be nothing in less experienced hands.

[23] Her name was Sarah Jane, and she could so an apple at two bites. She hadn't nice manners.

[24] They do say as there is to be a question asked about this in the House of Commons.

[25] I can swear that all this is true, for I took the letters.

[26] I have done the eighteen holes in ninety-two when no one was marking. The approach to the tenth hole is through thickly wooded country, and there are some nasty bunkers.

[27] Seventeen! I often did it in five.

[28] Milly often lay awake all night, I have heard her say, thinking out puzzles like this.

[29] Missus was the last one I would have took to be sentimental, but we all feels it at once time or another.

[30] I was in the kitchen mending Jane Annie's driver when they came to me. It was the last thing I ever did for Jane Annie.

[31] This was early in the term. Jane Annie saw the crumbs in Rose's bed and told Missus, and Rose had to write 1,200 lines of French, 100 for each tart.

[32] He brought the letter with him and handed it to her, but it was such an awful one that Missus made the collaborators promise not to print it.

[33] The band got five shillings between them from Missus to go away, but she had to pay extra for not taking the bull-pups.

[34] Tom has wrote another play since then for the Independent Theatre. It is about a baby that was tired of life and committed suicide.

[35] I had this catapult for bringing down the apples with.

[36] I pretended to go to the house, but when Tom wasn't looking I sneaked round to the boat-house and locked it and hid the key.

[37] I don't think Bab was so much in love as she pretended, she had always too good an "appetite." You should have seen how she tucked into the cold beef.

[38] They wouldn't let me get a word in, or I would have shown that of course the moral is No more good-conduct prizes.

[39] Bab and Tom are living happily ever after now, but Jack and Jane Annie doesn't hit it off very well. The Proctor said that those who didn't know no better would think that he had been made a fool of, so he went to live in London, and married Missus and they keep high class lodgers, and Sim is their manservant, to the disgust of Greg, who is now a lecturer in the University Extension Scheme. I am page at No. 4 now, and the Seminary is to be let or sold.

A Note About the Author

J.M. Barrie (1860–1937) and Sir Arthur Conan Doyle (1859–1930) were Scotland-born authors known for producing prolific works. As a child, Barrie was an avid reader who loved serialized stories. He went on to study literature at University of Edinburgh and wrote for the *Edinburgh Evening Courant*. Meanwhile, Doyle spent seven years at a Jesuit institution followed by a stint at medical school. Both men made their mark in publishing by writing bold and beloved characters that would stand the test of time. Barrie is best known for creating Peter Pan, while Doyle introduced the famous consulting detective, Sherlock Holmes.

A Note from the Publisher

Spanning many genres, from non-fiction essays to literature classics to children's books and lyric poetry, Mint Edition books showcase the master works of our time in a modern new package. The text is freshly typeset, is clean and easy to read, and features a new note about the author in each volume. Many books also include exclusive new introductory material. Every book boasts a striking new cover, which makes it as appropriate for collecting as it is for gift giving. Mint Edition books are only printed when a reader orders them, so natural resources are not wasted. We're proud that our books are never manufactured in excess and exist only in the exact quantity they need to be read and enjoyed.

bookfinity™

Discover more of your favorite classics with Bookfinity™.

- Track your reading with custom book lists.
- Get great book recommendations for your personalized Reader Type.
- Add reviews for your favorite books.
- AND MUCH MORE!

Visit **bookfinity.com** and take the fun Reader Type quiz to get started.

Enjoy our classic and modern companion pairings!

Classic & Modern